To Dan
the intellec.
friend

Who Is a Jew?

Who Is a Jew?

Thoughts of a Biologist

*An Essay Dedicated to the
Jewish and Non-Jewish Victims
of the Nazi Holocaust*

Alain F. Corcos

Who Is a Jew? Thoughts of a Biologist: An Essay Dedicated to the Jewish and Non-Jewish Victims of the Nazi Holocaust

Published by Wheatmark®
1760 East River Road, Suite 145
Tucson, Arizona 85718 USA
www.wheatmark.com

ISBN: 978-1-60494-719-9
LCCN: 2011944871

I would like to thank my friends Daniel Suits, Evelyn Rivera, and John Panayotou for their friendly criticisms of this essay; my grandson, Joel Heckaman, who is already an editor extraordinaire; and editor Peter Feeley, who had excellent suggestions that I included.

A Jewish physical type has never been preserved nor transmitted down to the present day, because such a type never existed; if such a type had existed it would long ago have been dissolved as a result of the subsequent intermixture of Jews with other peoples. What the Jews have preserved and transmitted have never been physical nor mental racial traits, but religious and cultural traditions and modes of conduct.

Ashley Montagu

MY PARENTS, MY BROTHER, AND I LIVED IN southern France under the German occupation from 1940 to 1944. Although we did not practice any religion—my father was very anticlerical—we were Jews (according to Hitler) because we had ancestors who were: we had Jewish blood. Therefore, we were destined to perish. My direct family survived, mostly because they refused to have anything to do with racial laws. However, I lost two uncles, two aunts, and two cousins in the death camps.

Not believing in Judaism did not prevent my brother, Gilles, and me from being victims of physical anti-Semitism. I vividly remember a day in the spring of 1940, before the capitulation of France. During a school recess, Gilles and I were on the school grounds when someone yelled, "Let's have fun attacking those Jews!" We put ourselves back to back and knocked down anyone who came near us. The fight was soon over. Many of our classmates did not know what Jews were and ran past

us. Others were friends of ours and did not participate in that kind of mean-spirited fun. Gilles and
I were not hurt, but we were scared as hell. Since
that day I have asked the question: Who is a Jew?

The Nazi's definition of a Jew was messy. If you
had three Jewish grandparents, you were racially a
Jew. However, if you had married a non-Jew, you
were spared death. Instead, you would be sent to
a labor camp. The Vichy government of France
(1940–1944) was more anti-Semitic than the Nazis
of Germany. According to them, you were a Jew if
you had only two Jewish grandparents and, sooner
or later, you were to be sent to a death camp.

In March 1944, Gilles and I, respectively seven-
teen and eighteen years old, escaped from France
through the Pyrenees and were jailed for a week in
Spain. We gained our freedom by being exchanged
for 200 pounds, each, of American wheat. General
Franco played both sides of the war because the
Spanish people did not have much to eat. We joined
the Allied forces in North Africa, and eight months
later we landed in America to be trained as air force
personnel.[1]

We saw the Statue of Liberty from our ship on

the day President Roosevelt was re-elected for a fourth term, but we did not see New York City at all. Immediately we took a train to the now-famous, or rather infamous, town of Selma, Alabama, a few miles south of Craig Field airbase, our destination. Two weeks after our arrival, Gilles and I got permission to visit Selma, and we decided to go to the movies. Being inexperienced with the customs of this country, we tried to go through the colored entrance. We immediately learned that in the United States we were members of the master race and had to use the white entrance.

A FEW MONTHS LATER I HAD THE CHANCE TO SEE New York, where it seemed that I was a Jew again. Although I was in an American uniform with a patch on my left shoulder with the word *France*, someone on the subway started to talk to me in Yiddish, a language I had never heard. Although the conversation turned to English, it was very short. A few nights later I was asked, in English, by a friend's Jewish neighbor if I were a Jew or a Frenchman. I thought, *what kind of question is that?* Being Jewish and being French are two different things. One pertains to religion, the other pertains to nationality. In my simple logic, one can be French and Jewish; French but not Jewish; or neither. I knew very well that this distinction was not made in the minds of the Nazi SS, but I was dumbfounded that the distinction was not made in the minds of some Jews as well. In the French Air Force, there was no anti-Semitism. They were all kinds of people, and we were all young and idealistic. Many, like Gilles and me, had volunteered for the duration of the war.

When the war was over I came back to France and headed the family flower farm. However, our methods for raising flowers were medieval. I decided to go back to the States to learn the modern techniques I was sure existed there. I landed in New York on my way to San Luis Obispo, California, where I was to be a student in horticulture.

In New York I found anti-Semitism from someone I did not expect. When I was in the French Air Force I met an interesting young woman named Elizabeth. We became friends. Two years later I called her up. (She was then a graduate student at Columbia University.) I asked her to meet me at the home of an uncle and aunt. Both were French but lived in the United States at the time. My aunt, thinking that Elizabeth was my girlfriend, asked her if she was Jewish. Elizabeth's smile disappeared. She clamored for an excuse and left—out of the house and out of my life. After that I did not experience any more personal anti-Semitism, neither when I was in college nor during my professional life.

ALTHOUGH MY DEGREES ARE IN BOTANY AND PLANT pathology, I became a geneticist. This was not news to one cousin, who told me, "You bothered all of us with your talk of genes and chromosomes when we were in high school." This knowledge of genetics reinforced my simple answer to who is a Jew— someone practicing Judaism. If not, one is not a Jew. My definition of a Jew is simple but, as I have learned, very far from being accepted. The question of who is a Jew depends on whom you ask. An orthodox rabbi gives you one answer, a reform rabbi another. An atheist sometimes gives two different answers, and scientists generally none because they tend not to think about unscientific classifications. However, I believe it is important to stress that biologically it makes absolutely no sense to talk about Jewish descent, because this implies that there are Jewish genes. There are no such things, as I will explain later in this essay.

My strong desire to write the present essay came after searching the Internet for the question, "Who is a Jew?" I could not believe the number of different answers I saw. Among the meaningless comments were that Senator Allen had a Jewish mother, John Kerry had Jewish grandparents, Howard Dean is married to a Jew, Dennis Kucinich was dating a Jew, Hilary Clinton had a Jewish stepfather, and Madeleine Albright had Jewish parents—something she did not know. Does it matter whether you are related to a Jew or are dating one? Does it make you a better politician? I do not believe it makes a difference, but obviously it is important to some people.

MOST OF THE COMMENTS HAD TO DO WITH religion and how it is interpreted very differently by orthodox and reform rabbis regarding Jewish descent from the mother's side, the father's side, or both. This discussion is baseless because it is contrary to the Scriptures.[2] If we say that to be a

Jew you have to have a Jewish mother, many sons of famous Jews, including Moses and Solomon, were not Jews.

There are very few comments criticizing the concepts of Jewish descent—being Jewish by birth—from a biological point of view, and those comments are generally poorly written and confusing. For example:

> [There] is a deeper issue here, and that is our changing understanding of the meaning of biological descent. After all, our theories of biology are more nuanced and complex than tribal notions of *blood.* The intellectual basis of equating patrilineal and matrilineal descent rests on the finding of *contemporary* biology. In an age of genome project, when we know for a fact that mother and father contribute equal shares of DNA, no one can argue that, biologically speaking, a child with a Jewish father and one non-Jewish mother is any more *genetically Jewish* than a child with a Jewish mother and a non-Jewish father.[3] (Italics added.)

We do not need contemporary biology to tell us how absurd an idea that is. We have known this for decades, since we first discovered chromosomes. Why does the author use the word *blood*? He destroys his own argument by saying "genetically Jewish." He should have added, "Children are Jewish or non-Jewish, not according to their genetic makeup, but because their parents want them to follow (or not follow) the Jewish rites."

O NE OF THE MOST VICIOUS MYTHS AMONG human beings is that there are human races.[4] For centuries, Jews have been considered a race—a biologically different human group. Before World War II, the Jews were referred to or thought of as a race, not only by laymen but also by many scientists, physicians, philosophers, politicians, and, of course, anti-Semites. The so-called "Jewish race" was generally characterized by a combination of physical and behavioral traits that rendered any member of it recognizable anywhere on earth.

The alleged characteristic physical traits of a Jew were held to be short-to-middling stature, a long, hooked nose, greasy skin, dark complexion, wavy hair, thick lips, flat feet, and a tendency for the women to be fat. The alleged characteristic behavioral traits consisted in a rather excessive allotment of the more unattractive social vices: aggressiveness, loudness, unscrupulousness, peculiar gestures (both of the hands and of the face), and a quality of looking and behaving in a "Jewish" manner—hard to define, but nevertheless real. The problem with these characteristics is that these human traits can found in any other population.

There are many people who claim to be able to distinguish Jews from all other people simply by the appearance that a Jew presents, even when only their back is visible to the observer. Once I had a Jewish student who claimed this ability, so I asked him to carry out a scientific experiment. He simply recorded how many times he was right or wrong in determining if someone who looked like a Jew actually was Jewish. My student was honest and, three weeks later, admitted that he had been right only 50 percent of the time.

DURING THE GERMAN OCCUPATION OF FRANCE, the Nazis tried to pick up Jewish children off the street, but a large number escaped detection, and many non-Jewish children were sent to concentration camps.[5] Many Jews who refused to declare their ancestry by changing their names and moving from one place to another also escaped their awful destiny. Some of them became members of the underground, and at least one became a member of the Gestapo. He saved many Jews by warning them before the SS or French police were on their way.

After the Holocaust, the concept of a Jewish race should have gone by the wayside. Although its emphasis decreased, it did not disappear. Strangely, there was a switch in who believed in the Jews as a race. Most non-Jews look upon Judaism simply as a religion and do not consider Jews as people biologically different from themselves. However, some Jews, priding themselves on being God's chosen people, jump to the conclusion that they must be biologically different from non-Jews, inventing Jewish "genes." To do so is to give Hitler a postmortem victory, for he and his cohorts built their hatred on the concept that Jews were a foreign, evil race to be destroyed.

In the last fifty years, anthropologists have demonstrated that Jews do not possess a community of physical characteristics that distinguishes them as a distinct ethnic group. Among them were Maurice Fishberg,[6] Karl Kautsky,[7] Ashley Montagu,[8] Harry Shapiro,[9] and Raphael and Jennifer Patai.[10] There is yet another book demystifying the Jewish race— mine.[11] In it I show that, historically and biologically, there were never conditions, such as isolation, that led to race formation. Jews have married non-Jews since the beginning. Non-Jews have become Jews and vice versa. Yet, such books do not influence the public's mind. They are little read, especially in Israel, where anthropological ideas that cast doubt on a distinct biological group called *the Jews* are practically never discussed.[12]

SHLOMO SAND, AN ISRAELI HISTORIAN, WROTE IN Hebrew *The Invention of the Jewish People*. It was translated first in French and recently in English. Currently the book is provoking a storm in the Jewish community by arguing that Jews have never been genetically or otherwise "a people." I agree with him, but he did not explain well enough why this is genetically true. To form a distinct biological human group (this is true for any organism), the group has to be isolated for many generations. This is not the case for the Jews, who throughout their history have married non-Jews, and many non-Jews have become Jews. A point that is not made at all is that the history of the Jews is the one only of Jews who remained Jews. What about the Jews who abandon the Jewish faith and marry non-Jews? Assuming that these Jews were biologically different from non-Jews, they would have transferred Jewish characteristics into other populations, decreasing any differences among them. According to a colleague and friend of mine whose father came from Spain and mother was Mexican American, all Spanish people have Jewish blood in their veins. He could have added that they also have Muslim blood and who knows what other type of blood. My friend, a biologist, knows that heredity is not carried in the blood, but I wonder how many of us still believe it.

As late as the 1980s, the United States Supreme

Court ruled that Jews were a race, at least for the purpose of certain antidiscrimination laws. Their reasoning: at the time that these laws were passed, people routinely spoke of the "Jewish race" or "Italian race," as well as the "Negro race," and so that is what the legislators intended to protect. But many Jews were deeply offended by that decision and by any hint that Jews could be considered a race. The idea of Jews being a race brings to their minds nightmarish visions of Nazi Germany, where Jews were declared to be not just a race but an inferior one that had to be rounded up into ghettos and exterminated like vermin.

I F JEWS ARE NOT A RACE, DO THEY SHARE THE same culture? Most American Jews think of their Jewishness as a matter of culture. They think of the food, of the Yiddish language, and of some holidays. But much of what they think of as a Jewish culture is just Ashkenazic culture—the culture of Jews whose ancestors came mostly from Eastern Europe in the last two centuries. They do not recognize that Sephardic Jews, whose ancestors came from Spain and its colonies, do not speak Yiddish—or that bagels, lox, chopped liver, latkes, gefiltefish, and matzah ball soup are part of their culture

I am reminded of a Jewish colleague, Marv Solomon, who, as an officer during World War II, found himself alone in the streets of a small Italian town that had been liberated just a few hours earlier. He did not speak Italian, and he was happy to see a house with a Star of David in a window. It was a strange display considering Italy was officially anti-Semitic under Mussolini.[13] Marv knocked at the door, and a man appeared. Marv started to speak to him in Yiddish, but got no answer. This Italian was a Sephardic Jew, someone who had never heard a word of Yiddish, but the man knew enough English to invite my friend to share a bottle of wine and celebrate freedom.

JUDAISM IS SPLIT INTO SEVEN PRIMARY DIFFERENT denominations: Ultra-Orthodox, Reconstructionist, Orthodox, Humanistic Conservative, Flexidox, and Reform. These branches differ from each other in some beliefs and, thus, in the way they observe Judaism. In this essay I will limit my discussion to only the differences between Orthodox and Reform Jews. (For example, they disagree about the content of the conversion process. The major disagreement between the orthodox and the more liberal denominations is over the need to accept the yoke of the commandments, which means making a lifelong commitment to orthodoxy. The Orthodox convert must be immersed in a ritual bath in the presence of witnesses, and men must be circumcised in the presence of witnesses. Such rituals are not obligatory for followers of the Reform movement, which emphasizes that the individuals make informed choices about their practice. The Reform rabbis are not obligated to perform conversions in any particular way.

The Judaism branches see the question, "Who is a Jew?" under a different light. Although Reform Judaism views Jews who converted to another faith as non-Jews, Orthodox Judaism considers children of a Jewish mother to be Jewish, even if they practice another religion or no religion at all. The descendants of a Jewish woman can claim to be Jewish, regardless of beliefs. A Jew who leaves Judaism is free to return to the faith at any time, with no formal ceremony or declaration required to return to Jewish practices.)[14]

I F ALL JEWS DO NOT HAVE THE SAME CUSTOMS, do they belong to a nation? The traditional explanation, also given in the Torah, is that the Jews are a nation. However, the term is not used in the modern sense, meaning a territorial and political entity, but in the ancient sense, meaning a group of people with a common history and destiny. It was in the modern sense that the French-Jewish community was considered a nation before 1789 a nation within a nation with its own laws. The French Revolution granted Jews citizenship, but they had to give up claims to national, communal, and judicial separateness.[15]

Today, Israel is politically considered a nation. But is it? Each Israeli carries an identity card that has a line indicating nationality, but instead of the word *Israeli*, the word is *Jew*. Are we back under the Nazi regime, when Jews wore a yellow star and their identity cards bore the word *JEW*? Israel cannot be a nation like the United States or France.

It is the Jewish state, even though many non-Jews live there and most Jews live elsewhere, where they are citizens of their countries. Israel is a state of, by, and for the Jewish people; its resources primarily benefit the Jews. Arabs are taxed like Jews, but they do not have the same access to resources as Jews. The land held by the state may not be sold or leased to Arabs, and Arab villages and farms do not get the same quality of services (electrical, water, etc.) as Jewish towns and villages.[16]

I F THE JEWS ARE NOT A NATION, ARE THEY A large extended family? In my experience, this seems to be true: Jews act like a large extended family. Like a family, Jews do not agree with each other. They argue and criticize each other. But, when someone outside the family unfairly criticizes a family member or the family as a whole, they are quick to join together in opposition. When members of the family suffer or are persecuted, they get help from other family members. Of course, this generosity is a human trait not restricted to the Jews. Corsicans, for example, fight among themselves when they are on the island, but when they are off of it, they act like brothers in cases of danger or injustice. When I was in the French Air Force, I was thought to be a Corsican, mostly because I have the southern French accent and use some similar expressions. One time, I was almost unjustly punished by a sergeant and was saved by a noncommissioned Corsican officer who thought I was his countryman. He told the sergeant, "If you punish Corcos, I will punish you."

THE WHO IS A JEW? DEBATE HAS BEEN A POLITical and legal minefield in Israel for five decades. Over the years, Israel's courts have repeatedly ruled that Judaism can take many forms, and that no form is necessarily entitled to primacy within the country. Israel's political system, however, has taken a different stance, granting monopoly on conversion, marriage, burial, and other personal status issues to the Orthodox rabbinate. The reason is purely political. While most Israelis aren't practicing Orthodox Judaism, few identify with other wings of Judaism, preferring to think of themselves as secular. And so, while the Orthodox community is a minority, it forms a solid political block. The liberal branches do not. The debate masks a monumental issue that many outside Israel underestimate. In no other democratic country is a religious qualification an official political matter.

Yet, even within Israel, there is a controversy over what Jewish state means. To some, the State of Israel was created to be a place where persecuted Jews can go, govern themselves, and be safe from anti-Semitism. To others, Jewish State means that the Israel government should incorporate Jewish traditions and customs in governing the state. To put it simply, there are religious Zionists and there are secular Zionists.

This controversy has been going on for a long time. Until the 1930s, Jews in the United States and Western Europe were largely uninterested in Palestine and Zionism. They did not see themselves as exiled from the Promised Land, and they did not seek a "return," despite a major effort to get them to think that this was their destiny. A German friend of my family went to Palestine in 1937, afraid of the racial laws that were instituted in her country. She quickly left Tel Aviv and came to New York City after discovering how religious Palestine actually was.

Israel was established as the Jewish State after World War II. The first problem was, of course, was "who is a Jew?" At first, anyone who claimed to be a Jew was considered a Jew. This suited most Israeli Jews, who were secular, but it dissatisfied the minority of religious Jews. Today, Israel recognizes only the Orthodox view as binding. The views of the other groups are deemed illegitimate. To be a first-class citizen of Israel, you have to be the child of a Jewish mother or have been converted by an Orthodox rabbi. This means that my wife's aunt, Helen, who married a Jew and converted to Judaism in a Reform ceremony in Indiana, would not be a Jewess in Israel.

Why does the Orthodoxy state that if their mother is Jewish, children are Jewish, but if the mother is a non-Jew, the children are regarded as non-Jews? There are two reasons for this position: First, the mother is thought to have a tremendous impact on her children, presumably because she spends the bulk of family time with them. Second, we can be certain of the maternity of a child,[17] but

not as certain of the paternity. These reasons are
social reasons, not logical ones. One is a Jew because
her mother is Jewish, who is Jewish because her
own mother was Jewish, which is a tautology. It is
not an explanation at all. And, as I said before, being
Jewish by birth is a very hard concept for biologists
to grasp because the only thing a mother gives her
child that is specifically Jewish is a religious envi-
ronment.

THE ANSWERING OF WHO IS A JEW? BY BIRTH HAS
led to irrational rulings. The child of a non-Jewish
mother who resides in Israel, serves in the Israeli
army, and lives in an atmosphere of Jewishness is
not considered Jewish. However, a child of two
Jewish parents who has no desire to participate in
or practice Judaism, who might not even believe
in God, is considered Jewish. In 1968, the Israeli
ministry of interior refused to identify Lieuten-
ant Commander Benjamin Shalit's two children as
Jewish because the mother was not Jewish. Shalit
argued that the government of Israel had no right
to use religion in judging nationality. He felt that
religious observance was not part of the concept

of Jewishness. After much debate and argument, the Israeli Supreme Court ruled in his favor. That decision lasted for only one day because of incredible opposition by one of the prominent, although small, religious political parties. The party threatened to topple the government by pulling out of the ruling coalition unless the court reversed itself. It did, which raises the question of how powerful and independent the Israeli Supreme Court is.

During the last two decades, the issue of who a Jew is as defined in Israel had become a major irritant in relations between that country and the American Jewish community. Most American Jews identify with the liberal branches of Judaism and consider the Israeli rabbis' obstinacy an insult to their faith. This obstinacy had cruel international consequences. A quarter of a million people from the former Soviet Union, victims of anti-Semitism, have flooded to Israel in the last century. They soon discovered that they could not get married or buried in consecrated Jewish soil.[18] According to senior rabbis, they were not "Jewish enough"; they were too liberal in their religious views. Today, many of them are leaving Israel.

A MACABRE STORY IS THIS ONE OF AN ISRAELI soldier, Lev Paschov, who immigrated to Israel under the Law of Return from the former Soviet Union. He was killed while on active duty in southern Lebanon in 1993, and he was buried twice. He was first interned in a regular Israeli military cemetery, but after it was discovered that his mother was not Jewish, his body was exhumed, and Paschov was buried a second time in a cemetery for non-Jews.[19] How can a government expect to stay unified if it makes such a distinction about its soldiers?

O RTHODOX JEWS BELIEVE THAT SOMETHING biologically Jewish is transmitted from parents to children. In the past they thought it was transmitted through the blood; today they think it to be through the genes.[20] In April 1996, the rabbi Yitzhak Ginsburgh went so far as to publish an article affirming that in each cell of a Jew—but not in those of non-Jews—there is a substance containing a part of God. According to him, the DNA of the Jews is different from that of non-Jews. This is the reason why we can transfer organs from non-Jews to Jews, but we cannot do the opposite.[21] I had never heard such a racist interpretation of the well-known biological phenomenon of organ rejection.

There is no doubt that, among Jewish geneticists in the past[22] and Israeli geneticists[23] today, there is a tendency to "prove" that Jews are biologically different—that they have different genes. The belief that there are Jewish genes is based on the fact that there is a genetic marker on the Y chromosome believed to be carried by the male descendants of Jewish priests. That is a very bad interpretation of what a genetic marker is.

Structurally, there is very little difference between a gene and a genetic marker; both are segments of DNA. However, a *gene* is responsible for a protein or other molecule, and these proteins and molecules have structural or physiological properties that contribute to the biologic functions of an individual. Any alteration in the DNA sequence of a gene may cause a protein to be incorrectly manufactured, resulting in a disease condition. On the other hand, *genetic markers* are specific locations in the DNA where there is known variability, but this variation has no physical effects on the individual. Genetic markers are used in genealogical reconstruction to trace a limited ancestry.

Many people are interested in their ancestry. Recently, they were told that complex genetic screening tests make it possible to determine where in the world their ancestors come from. Two main techniques are used: genetic markers on the Y chromosome can be mapped to trace paternal ancestry, or a similar process can be done on mitochondrial DNA to trace maternal lines. Both technologies take advantage of the fact that some genetic material is passed down, entirely unchanged, from parent to child—in the case of the Y chromosome from father to son, and in the case of mitochondrial DNA from mother to child (for both sons and daughters). This genetic technology, however, has severe limitations.

Mapping Y chromosomes and mitochondrial DNA will only trace two genetic lines on a family tree, where the number of branches doubles with each generation. Continue back in this manner for any number of generations and anyone will be connected to only one ancestor in each generation. The test will not connect him or her to any of the other hundreds, thousands[24] of ancestors to whom he or she is also related. This is a slender thread on which hangs an identity, especially in that tests also have a certain margin for error.

AMONG THE SEVERAL KNOWN GENETIC MARKERS IS the "Cohanim" chromosome, associated with last name *Cohen* or *Cohn*, traditionally held among Jews to be the descendants of Moses's brother Aaron. It is this marker that has been conceptualized as a Jewish gene. What does it mean if someone has this marker? Does it mean one is a Jew? Not necessarily, since men of Christian, Muslim, atheist, or any other belief, can also have this marker. The fact that non-Jews carry the Cohanim marker is not astonishing because, historically, there has been a tremendous number of men who have abandoned Judaism and married non-Jews. Their male descendants all inherited the marker. If you have it, it simply means that you might have a Jewish ancestor as far back as eighty generations.[25]

This did not prevent one rabbi, leader of the Ultra-Orthodox party, to decree that only people who are converted to Judaism—according to orthodox precepts—have the Jewish gene, while others do not. From a biological view, this decree is completely absurd. Genes do not suddenly appear after a baptism[26] or marriage.[27] There simply is no such thing as a Jewish gene,[28] only Jewish ancestors.

What bothers me most are the incredible generalizations that are made from genetic studies of the Y chromosome. For example, Nicholas Wade tells us in a *New York Times* article, "Studies Show Genetic Similarities of Jews," that two genome studies extend earlier studies based on the Y chromosome that Jewish communities existed in Europe and the Middle East some 3,000 years ago, even though each community also carries genes from other sources, usually the country in which it lives.[29] This is another example of a confusion between genetic markers and genes. More important, you can expect this type of conclusion for any population in the world. It would be far more important to have data that shows that Jews have certain genes that nobody else has. But, this is not the case.

Wade adds: "A major surprise from both surveys is the genetic closeness of the two Jewish communities, the Ashkenazim and the Sephardim.

The Ashkenazim thrived in northern and Eastern Europe until their devastation by the Hitler regime and now live mostly in the United States and Israel. The Sephardim were exiled from Spain in 1492 and from Portugal in 1497 and moved to the Ottoman Empire, North Africa, and the Netherlands."[30] How could this be a surprise? Jews marry Jews, whatever their origin. Before the wedding, they do not ask: are you originally from Spain or Russia?

In 2010, new research based on recent advances in genome technology confirmed that most members of the far-flung Jewish diaspora can trace their roots to ancestors who lived in the Middle East more than 2,000 years ago. Although we can track Jewish ancestry, it says little about who is a Jew today. The leader of one of two studies, Doron Behar, a geneticist at the Rambam Health Care Campus in Haifa, Israel, argues that "genes do not necessarily make the Jew. There is no metaphysical difference between [someone] born Jewish and a convert to Judaism." I agree, though I do not like, as I said before, the use of the term "born Jewish," which implies a biological ancestry.[31]

To me, these studies prove the obvious, and

they are not meaningful. I am at odds trying to understand what the actual purpose of this research was and why any Jewish people took part in it. I cannot prevent myself from thinking how ironical it would be that Adolph Hitler's DNA had the famous Jewish marker and Benjamin Netanyahu's did not.

M Y DEFINITION OF A JEW AS SOMEONE WHO follows the rites of Judaism seems very acceptable to non-Jews. However, my idea that "someone who does not is not a Jew" is rejected by Jews. Many, as I said before, believe that there is more to being a Jew than religion. In a discussion board, a woman posed the following question:

> My sister was baptized [Christian] and has since married and had a child. My mother claims the child is Jewish, but how could that be? If Judaism is a religion, if someone leaves it, she is no longer Jewish, right? [32]

The rabbi answered:

Logically, I would have to agree with you. If Judaism is a religion, then someone who doesn't believe in the religion should be no longer Jewish. The reality, however, is that it does not work that way.

The rabbi explained why by quoting the Talmud, the Jewish code of law, which confirms that the child of a mother who converts to another religion is still Jewish. I do not believe that the questioner was satisfied with the rabbi's answer, which relies on faith instead of logic.

The rabbi concluded:

Jewishness is about neither religion nor race. Unlike a race, you can get in, but unlike religion, once you're in, you can't get out.

One wonders where this man has been in his life to make the racist statement, "once a Jew, always a Jew." I doubt that such a statement exists in the Good Book. But, if we cannot leave Judaism, then there is a problem of freedom. After all, you are not born a Jew, Christian, or Muslim. You can be born in a Jewish, Christian, or a Muslim family. The same is true for your nationality. You are born in France, Egypt, or another country, because that is where your mother was. In both cases, it is an involuntary act. You do not choose your parents. However, once you are older, you have the freedom of nationality and religion—or lack thereof .[33]

T HERE WAS A GAP BETWEEN THE QUESTION AND the answer in the above example. But, there is a far greater gap between those who, as Jews, lived under the Nazis and those who read Anne Frank. The difference is "being there." It is the same difference between those who hear about wars and those who are on the battlefront. No matter how many pictures you see on TV and how many films you see of World War II or about the Holocaust, you have very little idea of what it was like to live through those catastrophes.

I remember that someone remarked after reading my book *The Little Yellow Train* (regarding my escape from France in 1944) that I was complaining more about having been considered a Jew than I was about the Holocaust. This man never had to worry about his life, being born in the United States after 1945. I, on the other hand, as a teenager, became a potential victim of genocide. It was perfectly natural for me to ask why I had to face death when others did not.

Young historians of the Holocaust cannot understand the emotional feelings and anxieties of those who were potential victims of the Gestapo (and, in France, also of the police)—always scared that at 5:00 AM someone would knock at the door and drag them in the unknown. I met one of those historians who showed his ignorance and lack of compassion as he was lecturing to students who had questioned me after reading *The Little Yellow Train*. I met another one at lunch one day who could not understand that I had been raised without religion. Obviously, he accepted the anti-Semitic idea that claimed Jews remained Jews, whatever they believed or did. The fact is that Jews, as other people, can renounce their religion or completely lose their faith in God at any time. I knew a Polish woman who survived the death camps. Liberated by American soldiers, she married one of them who was Jewish. She let her husband and her children go to the synagogue, but she stayed home, faithless and happy to be in the United Sates.

J EWS BELONG TO A RELIGIOUS FEDERATION—NO matter how loose it is. It is their religion that separates them from the rest of the world, not something biological. This was my belief when I was a young man under the Nazi regime. It did not change throughout my life—rather, it was fortified by my biology training. Yet today, twenty years after my retirement as a university professor, I am still upset when I hear someone telling me that Jews are more than a religious group, suggesting that a Jew remains a Jew no matter what he or she believes or does. It reminds me too much of the Holocaust and all the other genocides, which are carried on in the false belief that one human group is better, or even just different, than another.

By rejecting the notion of a Jewish race and Jewish genes and claiming that a Jew is simply someone who follows the Judaic rites, I am faced with a dilemma. How do I explain that there are some people, like some members of my own family, who are absolutely not religious but claim to be Jews? I believe their claim is based on a feeling of solidarity with the victims of anti-Semitism (in particular, those of the Holocaust). Whatever their reason, it is their choice and not the criterion of someone, like Hitler, who classifies them according to absurd pseudo-biological rules. If they want to be Jews, it is their choice. If I do not want to be a Jew, that is my choice. It is my right as a human being.

Endnotes

1 Alain F. Corcos. *The Little Yellow Train* (Tucson, AZ: Hats Off, 2004).

2 www.imhayim.org/Academic%20Stuff/Who%20 is%20%a20%Jew.him.

3 www.beliefnet.com/Faiths/2000/04/Jewish-Genes. Aspx?

4 Alain F. Corcos. *The Myth of Human Races* (East Lansing: Michigan State University Press, 1997).

5 Marc Hillel. *Au nom de la race* (Paris: Fayard, 1975).

6 Maurice Fishberg. *The Jews* (New York: Scribner, 1911).

7 Karl Kautsky. *Are the Jews a Race?* (Westport, CT: Greenwood Press, 1972).

8 Ashley Montagu. *Man's Most Dangerous Myth* (Cleveland and New York: The World Publishing Co., 1964) Chapter 16: "Are the Jews a Race?"

9   Harry Shapiro. *The Jewish People: A Biological History* (UNESCO: part of the collection *The Race Concept*,1960).

10 Raphael and Jennifer Patai. *The Myth of the Jewish Race.* (Detroit, MI: Wayne State University Press, 1989).

11 Alain Corcos. *The Myth of the Jewish Race: A Biologist Point of View.* (Bethlehem: Lehigh University Press, 2005).

12 Shlomo Sand,. *The Invention of the Jewish People.* (New York: Verso, 2009). 377

13 I said "officially," but in fact Italians saved a lot of Jews when they occupied the French Riviera where many Jews had taken refuge.

14 The requirements for conversions to Reform Judaism often vary from traditional ones. The denomination, the largest branch of Judaism in North America, states that people considering conversion are expected to study Jewish theology, rituals, history, culture, and customs, and to begin incorporating Jewish practices into their lives. The length and format of the course of study will vary from rabbi to rabbi and community to community.

15 Count Stanislas de Clermont de Tonnere, a revolutionary deputy is reportedly to have said in the French Assembly, "The French Jews should be denied everything as a nation, but granted everything as individuals."

16   Sheldon Richman. "Who Is a Jew in Israel?" *Washington Report on Middle East Affairs.* March 1990, p. 10.

17   I say "most of the time," because the woman might be the adopted mother.

18   Sheldon Richman. "Who Is a Jew in Israel?" *Washington Report on Middle East Affairs,* March 1990, p. 10.

19   http://danielGordis.org/2011/03/01/what-not-who is -a-Jew/

20   "Heredity of the Jews" was the first article in the *Journal of Genetics* in 1911. Redcliffe Nathan Salaman, a famous physician biologist, defends his thesis that according to which, even if the Jews do not constitute a pure race, they form, however, a compact biological entity. Not only can the Jew be recognized by the form of his cranium, his face, and his body dimensions, all these characteristics are due to one form of a gene.

21   www.letemps.ch/Page/unuid/e64bCb48.

22   Arthur E. Mourant, et al. *The Genetics of the Jews.* (Oxford: Oxford University Press. 1978).

23   Bat-Sheva Bonne-Tamir. "Analysis of Genetic Data on Jewish Populations." *American Journal of Human Genetics,* XXXI, 3, 1970, pp. 324–340.

24   The number of ancestors is limited since it grows exponentially. Sooner or later, it will be greater than

the number of people on earth, which means we have common ancestors and we are all related.

25 There are two interesting Y chromosome studies that confirmed oral tradition. One has to do with the descendants of Sally Hemmings, who claim that Thomas Jefferson was their ancestor. The other has lent credence that the Lemba, a Bantu-speaking people of southern Africa might be of Jewish descent.

26 After a lecture on the dangers of genetic diseases that affect many Jewish families of Eastern European origin, a student asked the teacher what the chances were that her child could have Tay-Sachs disease. "Are you Jewish?" the teacher asked. She replied: "Yes, since I married Bob."

27 When Catherine Elizabeth Middleton married His Royal Highness Prince William Arthur Philip Louis, she immediately became blue-blooded. Did her genes become another color?

28 John Dupre. "What Genes Are and Why There Are No Genes for Race." In *Revisiting Race in a Genomic Age*. Barbara A. Koening, Sandra Soo-Jim Lee & Sarah S. Richardson, eds. (New Brunswick, N.J: Rutgers University Press, 2008).

29 Nicholas Wade. "Studies Show Genetic Similarities of Jews." *New York Times*, June 9, 2010.

30 Ibid. Wade should have added France as another destination of the Spanish Jews.

31 "Who Are the Jews? Genetic Studies Spark Identity Debate." *Science*, June 11, 2010.

32 http://www.chabad.org/library/article_cdo/aid/129075/Jewish/Is-a-Jew-Who-Converts-Sti...6/11/2011.

33 You have the freedom of religion or nationality, but not of your skin color. As a former colleague told me, "A Jew can choose not to be a Jew. But, a black like me, cannot change my color." His color?

CPSIA information can be obtained at www.ICGtesting.com
Printed in the USA
BVOW030430020212

281919BV00001BA/8/P